MADE WITH 90% RECYCLED ART

A collection of
BASIC
INSTRUCTIONS
by Scott Meyer

BASICINSTRUCTIONS.NET

Foreword

By Missy Meyer

When Scott asked me if I would write the foreword for this book, I thought it would be easy. After more than thirteen years of marriage, I certainly have plenty of things to say about Scott. But that was the problem—too many choices. Should I write about his quirks and foibles? His writing process? His geeky tendencies (modern geek, of course; I've never seen him bite the head off a chicken—although one time he ate a Scotch bonnet pepper and staggered around the house imploring me to "feel the burn")? At least I didn't have to worry about the topic of his ghastly, soul-crushing hometown, since that was covered thoroughly by Scott's best friend Ric in the foreword of the first book (and probably even more in the afterword of this book).

I think, then, I will merely tell you about the little things that make Scott so awesome. He will always take the unwanted olives from your salad, and he'll always give you the pickle spear from his sandwich plate. He's a great slave to our feline overlords, even when they snub him or meow in his face in the wee hours of the morning. He will go out late, unasked, to buy the exact right kind of soup when you're sick. He'll go roller-skating, even though it terrifies him, because it's something you love to do. He'll give you his favorite pen, or the only cold can of root beer, or the last serving of ice cream. Scott will sit and watch "Down with Love" (again) with you, even though he'd rather be watching the new "Star Trek" (again).

But Scott is also good at the big things. He'll move across the country on very short notice, leaving everyone else he knows behind, so you can take that once-in-a-lifetime dream job. He's proven to be a champion when it comes to both sides of the vows: for richer or poorer, in sickness and in health. Whenever a big decision comes around, I can always count on Scott to tell me, "Whatever you choose to do, I support you."

Of course, as with any good artist, Scott doesn't see his own decent qualities too clearly. He worries constantly that he's not funny, that he's inconsiderate, that he's a complete idiot. We all know he's not, but he has trouble seeing that. The sincerity of his insecurity only adds to his charm and awesomeness.

Scott Meyer is, simply put, an easy guy to love. And to see someone so great find success in this comic, something he truly enjoys doing, delights me. Thank you, readers, for liking what he does. Because, in liking what he does, you're also liking who he is.

It's easy to overthink Rock-Paper-Scissors. Pick any of the three choices. They have an equal chance of winning.

In a tiebreaker, the item you chose first and the item that beats it should both be avoided as too obvious.

In a tiebreaker-breaker, don't take the one item you have not used. That's too predictable. Choose your original item.

In a triple tiebreaker, all bets are off. Pick any item. They have an equal chance of winning.

My wife and I have these marathon Rock-Paper-Scissors matches that stretch for four and five rounds. It's like watching ninjas fight ... with hand signals.

How to Converse with Someone You Don't Want to Talk To

Sometimes you just can't avoid getting stuck in a conversation with someone you don't want to talk to.

> Keep him occupied while we get the presentation ready.

> We hate each other.

> I don't think he hates you.

> He hates your behavior, attitude, and work ... but he doesn't hate you, necessarily.

Try to be pleasant and talk about things that are interesting. People like things that are pleasant and interesting.

> How're you doing?

> Better before you showed up.

> I'm not surprised. Primates often become agitated in the presence of a dominant male.

> That might explain my urge to "scent mark" you.

Try to find common ground. If you can find something you have in common, conversation will follow naturally.

> What do you do with your spare time?

> Loathe you.

> I do the same thing, depressingly enough.

> I don't find that depressing at all.

Of course, if you're successful, your reward will be talking to someone you didn't want to talk to to begin with.

> What do you loathe most about yourself?

> It's hard to say. Like trying to decide which of your children I like the least.

> You have kids?

> No, but you do, and I dislike them all equally.

I worked in an office for three years. More than once I had to stall clients while everyone else scrambled. I found cookies to be a useful tool toward this end.

How to Tell When a Cartoonist Is Getting "a Little Punchy"

Waking people up is easy to do by accident, but surprisingly challenging to do on purpose. Here are three ways.

Making a loud noise is easy and wakes your target all the way up, but is often considered discourteous.

A gentler method is preferred, but beware, even an attempt to gently wake someone up can startle them.

I suggest a passive approach. Think of something you do that wakes people up naturally and do it as if you don't know anyone's asleep.

When you find something you like, you want to share it with others. Sadly, others may not be as impressed.

I got a new phone!

You should call me on it to tell me about it.

I tried to! You didn't pick up.

Go try again.

Will you pick up this time?

No.

No matter how enthusiastic you are about something, you most likely won't be able to talk someone into caring.

Look, it's just a phone. When you die, nobody's going to say, "Scott had a really nice phone".

They will if I'm buried with it.

And I have an open-casket funeral.

Instead, you should try to find someone who has similar attitudes and share your enthusiasm with them.

Oh, that's awesome!

When I showed Luke, all he said was that at my funeral nobody'd care about my phone.

They would if it went off during the service.

PROMISE me that you'll call my phone at my funeral if you outlive me!

Whaddaya mean "if"?

In time, you'll amass friends who "get you," and who will take joy in the same kinds of things you do.

50 Years Later

He was a well-liked man...

As is demonstrated by the fact that his phone is still ringing off the hook even a week after his death.

BWANG BWANG BWANG

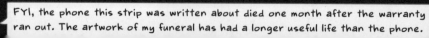

FYI, the phone this strip was written about died one month after the warranty ran out. The artwork of my funeral has had a longer useful life than the phone.

If you have an embarrassing middle name, don't hide it. Get it out in the open. I know this from experience.

My middle name is Oscar.

That's a cool name.

My last name is Meyer.

Your parents should be flogged.

The same questions will come up every time someone learns your middle name. Be prepared with answers.

I'm named after my grandpa.

Was he THE Oscar Meyer?

If he were, you and I would've never met, for I would be the Wienie King, and you'd be a mere subject in my empire of pork.

Instead of being embarrassed, try to frame your middle name as a positive thing that you're proud of.

I'd wear a kielbasa crown and wave my sausage scepter.

Ugh ...

Just picture it! The waving of the sausage scepter!

I'd really rather not.

If that doesn't work, try to steer the conversation away from your name and toward something distracting.

Six lucky kids would find a greasy golden ticket in their Li'l Smokies, and they'd get to come to see my sausage being made by Oompa-Loompas in gloves and rubber aprons!

I don't want to hear any more!

Then never mention my middle name again.

Yes, my middle name is Oscar. No, I don't have any funny stories about that. My middle name has never caused anybody to say anything to me that was funny.

If you're a lifelong *Star Trek* fan like me, you know you'll eventually be held captive by superintelligent aliens.

> I plan to study you by giving you everything you desire and watching your reactions.

> Fine by me.

> You'll have everything but freedom.

> I've had freedom. I'd like to try having the things I desire for a change.

One way to confound your captors is to fill your mind with primitive thoughts that they cannot understand.

> I'm probing your deepest desires. I see ... hot ... wings.

> Yes, you do.

> That's all? No beautiful women?

> A beautiful woman could bring me the hot wings.

If primitive thoughts fail, try confusing your captors with contradictory ideas and deliberately nonsensical illogic.

> Why do you value these hot wings so much?

> I like the heat.

> If it's a burning sensation you want, I'll give you the illusion of magma in your oral cavity.

> That sounds terrible!

> IT'S THE EXACT SAME SENSATION!!

Or you can teach them about humanity. If they understand you, they might not want to keep you imprisoned.

> I shall have to send you back to your planet. There's little I can learn from watching you eat fried food.

> What about my hot wings?

> HOT WINGS CAN BE HAD ON YOUR HOMEWORLD!!

> But they give me heartburn.

> BUT ... BUT ...

> Just go.

In the pilot for "Star Trek," aliens locked Capt. Pike up with a beautiful woman and simulated his fantasies. He tried to escape. I never understood why.

If you want a promotion, you have to be vigilant. A better job can become available at any time.

A job that sounds better than yours might not be. Investigate the new position to find out if you want it.

Once you're convinced the new job is one you want, find the proper person of authority and apply for it ASAP.

Even if you don't get the job, you'll have demonstrated that you want to advance, which is always a good thing.

These are instructions for how to talk loudly without yelling, not how to attribute your emotions to others.

You think I'm an idiot, don't you?

No, you think you're an idiot.

I AGREE that you're an idiot. There's a difference.

Speaking from the diaphragm makes your voice slightly louder and your words seem much more important.

I HAVE TO GO.

Where?

TO THE BATHROOM.

Oh. I thought it was something important.

IT IS IMPORTANT. I MUST GO NUMBER

I DON'T WANT TO KNOW WHAT NUMBER IT IS

The difference between projecting and yelling is largely one of tone. Maintain a pleasant, cheerful demeanor.

I'M GLAD YOU ALL CAME.

You don't look glad.

WELL I AM.

Now you look even less glad.

NOW I AM LESS GLAD.

Yelling is fast and incoherent. Speak in a slow, deliberate manner. As a result, you will seem confident.

Why'd you call us all here?

Yeah, we don't have all day to listen to your witless prattle.

I wanted to, uh, say that... um, you're all really good friends.

You don't sound sure.

No, I don't, do I?

Everyone in the group in panels three and four are members of my wife's former improv group. They were nice enough to pose for me, and I'm still punishing them.

It's hard to tell someone they have bad breath. You don't want to just say it, but subtle hints often won't cut it.

The easiest answer is to offer them a mint. Bad breath is the only problem that can be solved by eating candy.

Keeping your distance can be effective, but may just make them yell, spreading their bad breath further.

You may be forced to resort to the direct approach. If so, try to be sensitive to their feelings.

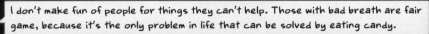

I don't make fun of people for things they can't help. Those with bad breath are fair game, because it's the only problem in life that can be solved by eating candy.

When someone tells you personal news, never assume news is good or bad. Find out their opinion before you commit.

My girlfriend's pregnant.

I see.

And you're ...

The father.

I see.

The human reaction to shock and horror is similar to shock and delight. This can be used to your advantage.

Isn't it great! I'm gonna be a daddy. Just think of it!

OH LORD! JEESH! OH MAN!

I know, right!?

Always be mindful of the other person's feelings. We all want to be honest, but now's really not the time.

Well I'm thrilled that ... you and the woman you refuse to marry are creating ... a ... hybrid.

Sorry, I just can't say it.

It's okay. I get all choked up at the idea of it too.

Yeah, I'm choking on something.

Interestingly, these instructions also work for the opposite problem. Someone telling you bad news that is actually good news.

She isn't pregnant. She'd gained some weight and I assumed the obvious. When I asked her about it she got mad and dumped me.

OH LORD! JEESH! OH MAN!

I know, right!?

How to Invent a Superhero

Start with your superhero's signature superpower. You'll find that inspiration for this can come from anywhere.

Did I ever tell you I once won a state fair axe-throwing contest?

No.

Pretty cool, huh?

Before I answer that, tell me this: do you have an axe right now?

Then, expand on that power. Try to think of ways it might be useful in your hero's fight against evil.

Axe throwing'd be a handy ability for a crimefighter.

Yes, there're few things that'll stop a purse snatcher as effectively as having an axe hurled into their back as they run away in a panic.

Now it's time to flesh out your new superhero's persona. Selecting a name is an excellent place to start.

What would you call a hero who fights crime by throwing axes?

How about "The Cold-Blooded Murderer"?

I was thinking of something more like "Axe Thrower."

Well, it is descriptive.

Once you know who your hero is, give some thought to his nemesis. Make sure they are as evenly matched as possible.

What kind of supervillain would be a match for "The Axe Thrower"?

"The Axe Dodger."

Ooh, I like that!

Sadly, I thought you might.

Two things. 1: It's wise to preface the answer to any question with "Do you have an axe?" and 2: Ric didn't win an axe-throwing contest. A woman I work with did.

It can be hard to make the transition to a balanced diet, but take heart. Healthy food doesn't have to be boring.

It's very important to read labels. Just because a product's package makes it look healthy doesn't mean it is.

Don't just find one or two foods you like and stick with them. Branch out! Variety is the key to healthy eating.

Be flexible. If a certain dietary approach isn't working for you, admit that it's not working and move on.

There are recipes available online for fried lettuce. Most of them are some variation on "Heat up some oil. Put some lettuce in the oil." Bon apétite!

How to Lose with Dignity

It's bad enough to lose a game without losing the respect of those around you as well.

Your attitude before playing a game is as important in saving your dignity as your behavior afterwards.

Be congratulatory to your opponent. Focus on your loss as a positive learning experience if possible.

Or you can play video games against artificial opponents who can't see your tantrums and don't care about your maturity level.

People often try to help each other. Being human, they often fail.

No matter how difficult they've made your life, try to remember, they were attempting to do you a favor.

Let them know how you intend to undo any damage they've inadvertently done and let them help if they wish.

If you can, you should forgive them and get on with the task at hand.

In society we're often made to thank people for doing things we didn't want them to do. The only consolation is that they say, "You're welcome," when we're not.

How to Proofread a Comic

The first step in proofreading a comic is to try to spell and punctuate everything properly in the first place.

"He plays the sousaphone."

Hmmm. Maybe I should write "tuba" to be safe.

Or I could just write "I am an ignoramus."

Hmmm. Maybe I should just write "dummy" ...

Once you're satisfied with your text, it's time to run the spell checker.

Replace Tubba with tubby.

Hmm. He plays the tubby.

Nah, fat jokes are beneath me.

You may be too close to the comic to see the minor flaws. It can be helpful to have someone else have a look.

Did you find anything wrong?

Yes, it's not funny.

But is there anything wrong with the words?

Yes. They're in a comic that isn't funny.

In the end, any mistakes you miss will be pointed out within five minutes of posting your comic to the Internet.

I got an e-mail that says I didn't draw a tuba. Apparently I drew a baritone.

Obviously!

I'll send him an e-mail saying he's right. I'll need you to proofread it.

Obviously!

Everybody's weird. Most people hide it. I say share your eccentricities with your friends, so they can enjoy them too.

Pick an eccentricity and describe it in a matter-of-fact manner, as if it's the most natural thing in the world.

Your friends will ask questions. Answer them honestly, maintaining the attitude that your actions are perfectly logical.

As they ask questions, more of your eccentricities will surface. Some may be more shocking than the first one.

It's true. I don't drink milk, because they squeeze it out of live cows. It just creeps me out. And yes, I love cheese. It comes from a factory, which is fine.

The best response to a request for an unreasonably large favor is a quick, polite but assertive no.

Say, can I — No.

You don't know what I was going to ask to do. — Doesn't matter.

Whatever it is, I know you can't.

I have great faith in your inabilities.

Decent people will take the no as the answer. Others will view it simply as the beginning of the negotiations.

Can I sleep in your spare bedroom for two weeks

Absolutely not.

How about your couch? — No.

Floor? — No.

Zip code? — No.

I already live in your zip code.

Without my permission.

Calmly explain why you are turning them down. This shows that you aren't refusing them for no reason.

I have a small place. We'd get on each other's nerves.

I wouldn't get on your nerves.

You're on my nerves right now.

Then I might as well come over!

Listen to them. If you won't give them what they want, you can at least show them the courtesy of hearing them out.

I need someplace to stay while my place airs out.

For two weeks!?

Yeah, you see ...

Before you tell me, ask yourself if the reason will make me more likely to have you in my home.

Never mind.

Most people fall into one of three categories. They make up the pointless game of Rock-Paper-Scissors we call "society." Pick the right one for you.

Tough Guy

Geek*

Suit

Tough Guy beats up Geek.

Geek fixes Suit's home network.

Suit puts Tough Guy in jail ... for beating up Geek.

Now that you've got a type, specialize. Pick a subset of your type and wrap your identity in it like a burrito.

I love "Star Trek"!

So, you're a Trekkie.

No, I'm a "Trekker."

What's the difference?

One "Treks." The other "gets Trekked."

Festoon yourself with the specific set of logos and licensed merchandise that proves your uniqueness to the world.

I rode my Harley in today.

So I see. Is that a new jacket?

Yeah. I had it custom made to show off my Harley tattoo.

Yes, I saw that it's cut out around your tailbone.

* "What about Jocks?" You ask. Jocks are just sports geeks. Live with it.

Seek out annual gatherings of people who share your interests and your passion for individual expression.

I'm doing Sturgis this year. It's gonna ROCK! Thousands of rugged individualists all gathering in one place.

Sounds great.

That's why I got the new jacket. My old one said "Honda" on it. They would've killed me if I'd worn that!

I'd been trying to make this idea work for a long time. I knew the idea of asserting your individuality by buying mass-produced Harley stuff (cont'd on next page)

It doesn't matter how good your job is, some part of it is bad enough that they have to pay you to get you to do it.

You wanted to see me?

No, I don't want to see you! I want to yell at you!

Just cower back there and listen!

Okay.

I DON'T WANNA HEAR YOU EITHER!

Complain to someone who has a better job than you do. If their job is worse, they won't sympathize at all.

He totally robbed me of my dignity.

Wow!

You had dignity!?

What was it like?

Ugh, it took lots of work to maintain.

Do not embellish your tale of woe. If it was really that bad, it won't need to be exaggerated to horrify your listener.

How long did he yell at you?

Ten minutes.

It must've been awful.

Yeah, but to be honest, he kept repeating the same five or six insults.

Towards the end, I was lip-synching along with him.

Don't lay it on too thick. Always bear in mind that if your job were really that bad, you would get a different job.

How can you stand this kind of abuse?

Well, it's on my terms. If it gets too bad, I can quit.

So, in a sense, "I quit" is your safe word.

Man, I wish that weren't true.

was funny, but how to do it without making bikers mad? Not because they'd beat me. Most bikers in Seattle were wealthy enough to have lawyers, which is worse.

If people complain about one of your public statements, respond with as much understanding as you can muster.

Mr. Meyer, you said that everyone is either a suit, a geek, or a tough guy. You then said that jocks are sports geeks. I think jocks may be tough guys who are good at sports. Signed, a fan.

Dear fan, HOW DARE YOU!!!

Listen to the opinions of those who disagree, then rationally weigh the merits of their ideas.

Maybe jocks are tough guys. Most of 'em can beat me up. Is that what makes a tough guy?

If it is, then you're married to a tough guy.

Heh, that's funny.

Is it really?

Uh, no ma'am.

If you find that some of the complaints are valid, then logic dictates that you rethink your position.

If a geek is just a person who's really into one specific thing, maybe tough guys are violence geeks.

I wouldn't want to be the one who tells them that.

And I sure don't want to go to their convention.

Once you've made the changes to your opinion that you've deemed necessary, be adult enough to admit it.

I realize now that a certain percentage of every subgroup in our society is passionate about sports.

It's just like homosexuality! They're gay for sports!

Perhaps you should keep this new theory to yourself for now.

WrestlMania is a violence geek's convention. The crowds look similar. The only real difference is that one crowd's happy to see Dwayne "The Rock" Johnson.

Manners are the veneer that prevents the knotty plywood of our society from splintering, and as such are necessary.

Manners are what lift us from the level of animals, so in general, the more natural something feels, the ruder it is.

If you want to really get serious about etiquette, there are a great many books available on the subject.

Proper etiquette is such a vast subject, even after diligent study you will still have much to learn.

Flashlights are one of those simple, utilitarian items that you don't think about until one lets you down.

I've had this flashlight a while, but it's old looking and kinda dim. Do you think I should get a new one?

A question I've asked myself many times.

There is a great variety of flashlight designs available. Shop around. Maybe a new model fits your needs.

It's head mounted. That way it points where I'm looking!

That'll make it easier to see everyone pointing and laughing at you.

There are also new technologies that can make modern flashlights more powerful and more energy efficient.

It's got like a hundred LEDs.

How long does the battery last?

Eight seconds, but the image stays burned into your retina for twelve hours!!

After you've examined your options, simply buy the flashlight that best fits your specific needs.

I got one that fits on my key chain.

It's not very bright, or useful, but it'll always be with me.

Reminds me of ...

Ugh. When you make it this easy, it ruins the fun.

The first step in finding a job that suits your interests is to identify what your interests are in the first place.

> I need to find a job doing something I'm good at, but what?

> Fleeing like a coward?

> Are you referring to jogging? I do that for my health.

> Which is fleeing like a coward from your own mortality.

Then list the jobs that fit those interests. Unfortunately, many of the obvious answers will be impractical.

> People run from the police. Maybe there's money in that.

> I'm not a criminal.

> You'd run for the criminals.

> What, and carry them on my back?

> Don't be ridiculous. I suggest you use a rickshaw.

In order to find a job that fits both your interests and reality, you might be required to think "out of the box."

> Skaters make a living performing in shows. Is there something like that for runners?

> What, some sort of "TrackCapades?"

> Yeah! Sprint of the sugar plum fairies! Jumping flaming hurdles! That kinda thing!

Once you've identified the job you want, you'll have to make it happen, which is often the hard part.

> You could always found it yourself! All you need is a fairy costume, hurdles, and gas!

> You just want to see me injured and humiliated.

> Many people do, and that's a market you can exploit!

> And be exploited by.

Before you make an analogy, be aware that some comparisons are inherently offensive, regardless of your message.

Word your analogy succinctly. Brevity is the soul of wit, so much so that it's often mistaken for wit itself.

Try to draw comparisons with things that will evoke an immediate, visceral response from the listener or reader.

A good analogy is a powerful tool, in that it seems simple but reveals a larger truth.

I've always been good at analogies, but analogies are like odors, in that I make too many of them, and others are never as impressed with them as I am.

There are few people that you want to insult, but sometimes you have to insult somebody for their own good.

One way to avoid offending someone is to phrase the insult so that it can be mistaken for a compliment.

Beating around the bush will only serve to prolong the insult-delivery process. It is always best to be direct and firm.

You could employ a preemptive faux apology, like "With all due respect," to head off hurt feelings at the pass.

Music's hard to discuss. Everybody thinks their opinions are right and are shocked to learn that others disagree.

People feel very strongly about their musical tastes, so make sure your criticisms are fair and well thought out.

Even if your point seems completely self-evident, you might have to defend your position, so be prepared.

The beauty of the discussion is that you learn—either about the subject, the person you're talking to, or yourself.

Talking to people who speak another language can be frustrating. Even the simplest exchanges become difficult.

> Please have a seat.

> ¿Qué?

> Please ... sit.

> ¿Qué?

> If it's "okay," why won't you sit down?

> ¿Qué?

Make every effort to speak clearly. Pronounce words fully; speak in a loud, clear voice; and avoid extra words.

> Perdóneme, no hablo inglés.

> I'm sorry, but I don't speak any Spanish.

> NO HABLO INGLÉS.

> I DON'T SPEAK SPANISH.

> HABLAR FUERTE Y LENTO NO AYUDA.

SPEAKING LOUD AND SLOW DOESN'T HELP.

If you happen to know any words in their language, use them. It will add clarity, or at least show effort.

> What was it Hernandez used to call me? He said it meant "good friend." OH YEAH!

> Agujero de tapón.

> ¿Agujero de tapón?

> ¡AGUJERO DE TAPÓN!

> ¡¡AGUJERO DE TAPÓN!!

> I've made a friend!

Be patient. Remember, your actions will help this person form their impression of your entire country.

> Turns out it meant "bung hole."

> I left him with the impression that Americans are loud, slow witted, and foul mouthed.

> He's just one guy. It's not like all foreigners feel that way.

> Yeah, thank goodness.

Turns out there is no word in Spanish for "bung hole." I'm told the phrase above translates roughly to "hole for a stopper," which misses certain subtle nuances.

If, like most sci-fi fans, your speech is made up mostly of movie quotes, you'll often find gaps in others' knowledge.

Soylent Green is people.

What's that even mean?

It's from a movie. I'll tell you about it. It's horrible.

That's not much incentive.

And then I'll never mention it again.

SOLD!

Being used to the glossier science-fiction films we have now, they will be shocked at what sci-fi used to be like.

Then he yelled, "SOYLENT GREEN IS PEOPLE!"

That's it?! He didn't fight aliens or anything?

Not in the '70s. Back then, man fought his own self-destructive tendencies, and sometimes apes.

Did man beat the apes?

Of course not.

Describe several old films to make it clear that it wasn't just one isolated movie that was a total bummer.

Didn't any movies have happy endings back then?

Richard Dreyfuss abandoned his family at the end of "Close Encounters of the Third Kind."

That made him happy?

It made his wife happy. She'd kicked him out already, because he'd lost his mind.

Sharing knowledge is its own reward. It is always rewarding to see others gain knowledge, and perhaps wisdom.

Well, I gotta get back to work. The boss has been a jerk lately.

Yes, we must all kneel before Zod.

What?

It's from a movie. I'll tell you about it. It's horrible.

No thanks. I think I'll be happier not knowing what you're talking about.

"Silent Running": Hero kills himself. "Rollerball": Hero kills opposing team with bare hands. "Death Race 2000": President David Carradine. Do I need to continue?

The only two ways to keep a secret are to tell no one, or to make the secret so idiotic, nobody will care enough to tell.

If part of your secret slips out, shut up immediately. Saying more isn't going to make them less likely to tell.

If the secret is worth telling, and somebody else knows, you may have to take extra measures to keep it quiet.

If you must tell someone, don't pick a happily married man. He will tell his wife. That's why he's happily married.

I've said it a million times, and I'm going to keep saying it until people start listening. A man can hold onto his hair, or his dignity, but not both.

The opportunity to introduce two people you know to each other for the first time often comes as a surprise.

State the two people's names and how you know them as simply as you can.

They both know you, so it follows that they may have other mutual friends or shared interests.

It can be strange when people from different parts of your life meet, but it's rewarding to see people connect.

Mr. Ryan is modeled on a guy named Ryan. He's much taller than me, so shrinking him to my size makes his brainpan look tiny, which works for the character.

Never be ashamed to take a nap. It's been proven that a good nap can actually increase your productivity.

To nap successfully you'll need a dark, quiet, comfortable place. If none is available, you can simulate one.

It's best to nap somewhere away from other people. They can be a distraction and make you feel self-conscious.

Naps are pleasant, but beyond that, your increased energy level will be more than reward enough.

It would be impossible to hold a "World's Laziest Man" contest. Anyone who showed up to compete would have to be disqualified.

First, in order for your analysis to be worthwhile, you must come up with a unique and original observation.

"Moby Dick" is the greatest American novel ever written ...

... about marriage.

Use the plot of the classic work you're analyzing to demonstrate your idea.

Ahabs killed many whales, but then a whale eluded him.

The whale played "hard to get."

Ahab became obsessed. He ignored other whales. Ahab was now a "one-whale man," if you will.

Also note that the whale wore white.

If the idea is sound, you should be able to match the entire plot to your concept without the idea falling apart.

When he finally found the whale, he lashed himself permanently to the whale's side.

Then the whale got rid of Ahab's friends and his boat.

Before unleashing your analysis, make sure you have an audience that is receptive to radical new ideas.

Wow! That's ...

Brilliant?

Sexist. Really $$#*ing sexist.

We can't judge Herman Melville. It was a different time back then.

I promise, I'm not judging Herman Melville.

This is "the Moby Dick bit." It is the best thing I ever wrote as a stand-up comic. Most of my fellow comedians were amazed that it was actually about a whale.

36

It used to be that spoiling the plots of TV shows for people wasn't an issue.

But now shows have such intricate story arcs that it's hard to discuss them without ruining it for others.

Before even discussing the plot, try to figure out the last episode they saw. This will help you avoid "spoilers."

If you can't pinpoint the last episode they saw, keep all discussion as vague as possible.

 No, Ric is not really a Right Said Fred fan. Yes, that is what our hair used to look like. No, I really don't think losing mine was much of a loss.

These are not instructions for how to suck up. You already know how to do that, and how effective it can be.

Boss, you're a good-looking man.

And you're a suck-up.

Well she's your new supervisor. Whaddaya think of her now?

That she's a good-looking suck-up.

Remember, you depend on many people who are not your superiors. If they feel unappreciated, you will suffer for it.

Did you get me that RJ-17 form?

Nope.

Why not?

Because you reward people for flattering you, not for doing their jobs well.

So flatter me.

Ugh, it's easier just to get you the form.

Find something your underling has done well and praise them for it. As long as it is honest praise, it'll be appreciated.

Hey, I liked how you got me the RJ-17 form.

You mean "slowly, and with a bad attitude"?

No, I mean "without making me threaten to fire you."

Well, I aim to please, to a very small extent.

And don't confine your "sucking down" to your employees. Anyone serving you will probably enjoy some praise.

I told your boss that you've finally learned to admit your ignorance and keep your fat yap shut.

I don't know what to say to that.

That's the stuff!

I'm not good at sucking up. I am pretty good at treating managers and executives with respect, which is seen as sucking up by those who don't share that skill.

How to Talk to a New Parent

Most people have difficulty thinking of things to talk about. New parents don't have that problem.

> Did I tell you that my baby said "PA PA"?

> Yes, you told me last week.

> No, last week I told you he said "BA BA." This week he said "PA PA." He's growing up so fast.

> Yes. Agonizingly fast.

Be complimentary. Their baby is the most important thing in their lives, so try to find something nice to say.

> He loves to tug on my finger.

> You taught him the "pull my finger" game so young?!

> I didn't teach him the "pull my finger" game!

> Then you may have a prodigy on your hands!

If they talk about aspects of baby care you don't want to hear about, you can change the subject by asking questions.

> Is your husband the father?

> YES!

> So you chose to pass on his negative traits?

> What traits?

> I've already said too much.

> I agree.

Relate their baby to your experiences. This shows that you're listening and engaged in the conversation.

> You never know when the baby will cry or spit up or wake you up in the middle of the night.

> Babies are like cute little alcoholics.

> That's not true!

> You're right. They're not all cute.

"Pull my finger: A strange game. The only winning move is not to play." "War Games" would have been a very different movie if I had written it.

39

How to Apologize When You're Not Sure What You Did Wrong

We seldom set out hoping to offend people. As such, we often offend people without knowing how we did it.

> You need to apologize to our biggest client.

> Again? What's the point? He knows I don't mean it.

> My girlfriend knows I don't enjoy musicals, but she enjoys making me pay to go see them.

> Touché.

Ask what you did to offend the person. This shows that you're concerned, and that you didn't offend them on purpose.

> I'm told you want me to apologize.

> I'm sure it's just a misunderstanding.

> You called me an idiot. That's hard to misunderstand.

> For smart people, yes.

Discuss the specifics of the situation. You may be able to demonstrate that you honestly meant no harm.

> I already said I was sorry.

> You said you were sorry I was born an idiot.

> And I truly am.

Once you understand how you offended them, apologize as sincerely as you can without lying or patronizing them.

> I'm sorry you're an idiot.

> Try again.

> I'm sorry I told you that you're an idiot.

> Nope.

> I'm sorry that I was so insensitive to your feelings and that I insulted you.

> You idiot.

> SO CLOSE!

Mullet Boss is an amalgam of the negative traits of everyone in my life, occasionally even me. For instance, I paid good money to see "Starlight Express."

It seems like every day more bits of information get thrown at us. Bits of information we need to retain.

Learn as much detail as you can. The better you understand something, the more memorable it becomes.

If you can't recall the information when you need it, relax and think. Panicking won't help you remember.

Don't worry if you can't remember. This failure will make the information more memorable next time you need it.

Everybody feels old occasionally. I mean everybody.

> I am not looking forward to my birthday this year.

> I'm gonna be twenty-three.

> On your twenty-first birthday, you drink because you can. Every birthday after that, you drink because you must.

Nobody likes the feeling of being old, but that feeling is like energy, which science tells us can't be destroyed.

> Your whole life's ahead of you.

> Except for the quarter of it that's behind me.

> The average life expectancy is seventy-five. A third of it's behind you.

> That doesn't make me feel better.

> Statistics seldom do.

Also like energy, the feeling can be transferred or converted. "Feeling old" can be transferred to someone else.

> Suddenly I just feel much older.

> Like the guy at the end of the third Indiana Jones movie who aged all at once.

> I don't remember. I saw that movie when I was four.

> You disgust me. And so do your parents, come to think of it.

Negative feelings about being old can be converted into positive feelings by relentlessly ridiculing the young.

> He's twenty-two and he feels old.

> Stupid punk kids.

> I know! They kill me.

> Whaddaya mean "they"?

> I'm not a stupid punk kid! I'm in my thirties!

> So you're a middle-aged stupid punk kid. That's the worst kind.

How to Reveal a Shocking Truth to a Person Who's Not Ready for the Truth

People are not accustomed to hearing pure truth, and as such, their minds must be carefully prepared.

Today I have realized a shocking truth. Would you like to hear this truth?

Yes.

Are you sure you're ready for the truth?

Yes.

'Cause I'm gonna truth you up!

Okay, maybe I'm not ready.

You can't hit them with all of the truth at once. You must portion out the truth in small, slightly less shocking chunks.

This truth pertains to the Muppets.

Okay, now I'm pretty sure I don't want to hear it.

Once their minds are well primed, you can hit them point blank with both barrels of your truth gun.

The truth is that the Muppet you know as "Beaker" actually spoke perfect English. The sound you think of as his voice is just the sound that the censors used to cover up his incredibly foul mouth.

Their minds will naturally rebel from that much truth. You will need to prop up the truth with hard evidence.

MEEP MEEP MEEP MEEP MEEEEEP, MEEMEEP MEEP MEEP!

(sigh) The truth, I suppose.

I grudgingly admit, you might be on to something.

And just what might I be on to?

YES, THAT'S RIGHT! THE MEEPING TRUTH!!

I've always loved Beaker. Picturing him constantly cursing hasn't changed that. Indeed, it has added a new dimension to his relationship with Dr. Honeydew.

43

How to Defeat a Lie Detector

As our society grows increasingly paranoid, many organizations consider the lie detector an indispensable tool.

Three reams of paper were stolen.

Yes.

So you rented a lie detector to find the culprit. Is that really cost effective?

YES!

Would you say that if you were hooked up to the machine?

Lie detectors measure stress. Thinking about stressful things will cloud the results like a flop-sweat smoke screen.

If I fail this test, he'll fire me.

I'll lose this job. I'll be unemployed.

Excellent! Your blood pressure is going down.

A more subtle method is to only say things that are true. If you believe something is true, it is not a lie.

I took the paper.

I'm making a papier-mâché statue of you.

That's disturbing.

The staff and I plan to burn it.

Still disturbing, but in a different way.

If you can make your interrogator distrust the lie detector, it won't matter if your lies register or not.

I get the point. If it didn't catch any of those lies, it's useless.

Uh, YEAH! That's my point exactly!

BZZZ

The machine doesn't work.

BZZZ

I've tried to avoid making this type of comment, but I have to ask, WHAT THE HELL'S WRONG WITH MY FACE IN PANELS TWO AND THREE?!

44

Often in life you will encounter a task that seems needlessly complex.

It is easy to get hung up on unrealistic solutions, but it doesn't matter how appealing an idea is if it won't work.

Analyze the process you're trying to simplify. Try to find those elements that are causing it to bog down.

Once you've identified the problem or problems, all that is left is to take positive action to eradicate them.

I know what's wrong with my face in panel two of this strip. That's just how I look when I brush my teeth. Haven't had much more need for that drawing, oddly.

When someone you know is depressed, it can be hard to know what to say.

I'm depressed.

I'll bet.

I mean, of course you are.

I mean ...

I'm sorry to hear that.

You'll want to say something to make them feel better, but you should always start by listening.

Tell Daddy what's wrong.

Well, I have a friend who's asking me to call him Daddy, for one thing.

Once you know what's bothering them, try to sum up how they're feeling. This will show that you understand.

I know. You feel like God is a garbage man, and your life is his landfill. And sometimes, if you listen with the right kind of ears, you can hear the dump truck backing up.

Just listen.

Do you hear it?

BEEP BEEP BEEP BEEP

It can be trying, but when your efforts succeed in easing someone's pain, it is always tremendously rewarding.

BEEP BEEP BEEP BEEP BEEP BEEP
BE STOP SAYING BEEP!!! P
BE P
BEEP BEEP BEEP BEEP BEEP BEEP

Will that make you happy?

Happier than I am right now.

Then my work is done.

Goodbyes are often awkward and painful. Sadly, they cannot be avoided.

I'm leaving for a better job. Is there anything you'd like to say?

Not until after you leave.

Are you afraid of embarrassment?

No, reprisals.

Though the feelings dredged up by people leaving are often powerful, it is best to avoid big emotional scenes.

I always promised myself that when this day came, I wouldn't cry.

You're not crying. You're smiling.

I never promised I wouldn't smile.

If you have mixed feelings or negative feelings about the person leaving, it is still important to say something nice.

You will be ... um ... "missed" ... by ... everyone ...

else.

Make sure that this is really goodbye. Nothing's worse than saying goodbye, then having the person stick around.

I've convinced her to come back! I didn't even have to offer her a raise!

She wanted to be my supervisor, didn't she?

She said she wanted "opportunity for reprisals," but functionally it's pretty much the same thing.

 The word missed is in quotes, and I'm making quote fingers. That means it's a double quote, a grammatical construct I invented just now, to cover for myself.

47

Correcting a coworker who is making a mistake is the right thing to do. It's not the easy thing to do, unfortunately.

Discuss the situation to find the source of the problem and identify solutions.

Solving the issue may require some creativity on your part.

Correcting a coworker is not fun, but the results are a productive workplace and a reputation as a problem solver.

To understand how Democrats interact with Republicans, imagine you're in a room with a person you think is crazy.

To minimize your discomfort, you avoid contact with the person you don't understand. This seldom fosters trust.

After a long, strained silence, every exchange will take on a hostile edge.

Sadly, the lack of communication makes it impossible to really know what the other party is truly thinking.

Life is a series of problems, and often you see the problems coming, which results in feelings of dread.

Give the situation some thought. Try to figure out what specifically is the cause of your anxiety.

Of course, if you're really dreading something, you will be tempted to hide from it.

Hiding from things you dread makes you dread them more. Better to face your dread and get it out of the way.

"Aggro" could also be an abbreviation for "Agricultural." Given the attitude of many of the farm kids I grew up with, the meaning of the insult wouldn't change.

Making your voice sound spooky is not difficult. Simply speak lower, slower, and louder than you usually would.

HELLO, RICK!

Why are you talking like Santa?

But you'll find that when trying to sound spooky, what you say is more important than how you say it.

BEWARE, RICK!! I SHALL BRING A DIRE TORMENT UPON YOU!!

What, are you gonna give me a lump of coal?

If you're dressing up in a spooky costume, choose one that fits your specific spooky voice.

Why did you come to my Halloween party dressed as Santa?

BECAUSE THIS COSTUME IS A VERY CHEAP RENTAL THIS TIME OF YEAR.

Work on spookifying your whole spooky package. The whole is often spookier than the sum of its spooky parts.

THIS ISN'T EVEN THE WHOLE OUTFIT! WAIT TILL YOU SEE MY SACK!

UGH! Jeez, you're so creepy!

I'm sorry my voice scares you.

It has nothing to do with your voice.

Yes, Mullet Boss is dressed as Sean Connery's character in "Zardoz." For the record, "Zardoz": Hero kills immortals (?!) then dies of old age.

If you are honest with yourself, you will have to admit that you could stand to improve yourself in many ways.

I still have a lot of room for improvement.

True.

I thought you would disagree.

You can start improving yourself by lowering your unrealistic expectations.

One popular means of self-improvement is to expand your horizons. Try new things, or learn a new skill.

I will watch "Iron Chef," then cook and eat one of the dishes.

Today's secret ingredient is ... PIGLETS!

Tomorrow.

If your problems are either physical or mental in nature, medical science may hold the answer.

HEY! HEY!

Sorry, I had my eustachian tubes tied. Now I can't hear kids.

That makes no WHAT?

It doesn't work that WHAT?

Don't tell other people about your self-improvement. They don't want to hear about your problems, or lack thereof.

I have shed all of my human weaknesses.

I assume you considered hair a weakness.

Yours certainly is.

Piglets were the actual ingredient on an episode of the original Japanese "Iron Chef." Yukio Hattori unveiled the ingredient in a hilariously apologetic manner.

Song lyrics are often quite abstract, and as such can confound even the most careful listener.

Try to identify which elements of the song are confusing you.

Once the confusing elements of the song have been identified, analyze them rationally.

Remember, music is to be enjoyed. Overanalyzing a song may ruin it for you, and those around you.

People express their identity through their clothes. For American men, that often means wearing a printed T-shirt.

T-shirts are a popular gift, which can be a problem in that the ideas expressed are those of the giver, not the wearer.

There are now many services you can use to create truly unique, one-off T-shirts that you've designed yourself.

Putting thought into your clothes, even a T-shirt, tells the world you care about your image, which is always good.

First find a seemingly intractable problem. You won't have to look far. We have more than enough of them.

Global warming isn't man made.

You don't believe it's caused by fossil fuels?

Of course it is, but man didn't make fossil fuels.

HA! EAT LOGIC!

Refine the problem, making it less abstract and easier to comprehend.

You realize that we will run out of oil eventually.

But it'll get super expensive first, lowering demand.

Because only the rich will be able to afford it.

That'd worry me terribly, if I weren't rich.

Once the problem is defined, explore alternatives logically and practically.

Well, what did we use for fuel before gas?

Sperm oil, for one thing.

That's disgusting.

It's not what you're thinking. It came from whales.

UGH!!

They killed sperm whales and made oil from their bodies.

Oh, that's better.

Really?

Often innovative answers come in a sudden insight that wouldn't have happened without thorough analysis.

Well there's your answer! Whales are a renewable resource.

Are you suggesting a whale farm?

No, I'm suggesting a whale ranch. It sounds manlier.

Ride 'em, Whaleboy.

I once said that children were our most precious resource, so I'd built an engine that got twenty miles per child. Whale ranch doesn't seem so bad now, does it?

55

Every now and then when I'm writing a strip, an extra joke will occur to me. There's seldom room to shoehorn the extra joke into the strip, so it ends up being a private joke for me. What follows is an epilogue to "How to Travel Back in Time to Issue a Dire Warning to Your Former Self." The characters are me as a teenager, and me from the future.

Enjoy.

So, what's with the codpiece? Are we the lead singer in a Cameo cover band, or what?

In the future everyone wears these. They're to shield the radiation.

There's so much radiation in the environment in your time that you have to protect your genitals from it!?

No, there's little radiation in the environment in the future because we protect it from our genitals.

I can only take the codpiece off if you wear a welding mask.

Ah, that is the purpose of the goggles.

Indeed.

 I'll level with you here. This joke had been rattling around in my skull ever since I first drew that codpiece, and I made this comic just to get rid of it.

To clarify, this guide's not about accepting compliments about you, directed at someone else.

Tell your boss he has an excellent ...

Lackey? Minion?

What are you?

I like to call myself his lickspittle. I'm kinda old school.

These instructions refer to when a person wants to compliment someone who's not there, so they say it to you.

Your friend Rick is cute.

I assume you're being sarcastic.

No.

Or you're being condescending. Like when someone is an idiot, and people say they're adorable.

No! I meant it. He's cute.

Did you wink, or cross your fingers?

Whether you agree or not, accept the compliment graciously and move on.

So by "cute," you mean ...

Attractive.

And by "Rick," you mean ...

Rick.

I see.

That's adorable.

Then when you next see the person who has been complimented, pass the compliment along to them.

Did she wink, or cross her fingers?

No! I checked!

Wow! I'm cute!

Don't let it go to your head.

Why should I listen to you? You're not cute, like me.

No, but I'm an excellent lickspittle.

It doesn't matter how peaceful a person you are; we are all occasionally seized by the urge to kill.

When the blood lust grips you, take a moment and count to ten. This gives you time to calm down and think.

If counting didn't quite do it, think of someone you admire, a role model of yours, and ask yourself what they'd do.

We all know you're not going to kill anyone, but you need to find your own reason not to kill.

This entire strip was built around the idea that in times of stress I would ask myself, "What would Emperor Palpatine do?" Sadly, the answer is "lose eventually."

Pets are unreasoning animals, and will exhibit undesirable habits. These habits can be eliminated.

In order to stop your pet's bad habit, firm and effective discipline must be administered immediately.

The discipline must be consistent. The pet must know that negative behavior will always receive the same response.

If you have enough willpower to follow these steps, your pet's positive behavior will become locked in place.

Enthusiasts of any medium (comics, in this case) will feel that artists in said medium have made mistakes.

I stopped caring about Green Lantern when they gave Hal Jordan fear.

His whole deal was that he was "the man without fear."

Who wants to read about "Hal Jordan, the man crippled by fear"?!

It's easy to take these things far too seriously. Try to keep it fun. Explore any idea, no matter how silly.

I understand why they made Green Arrow's sidekick a drug addict, but why heroin?

His name was "Speedy." Wouldn't uppers make a lot more sense?

Maybe he needed to take the edge off.

Think big. It can be interesting to rethink major aspects of your subject, imagining how those changes play out.

The Hulk's story is so much sadder if you tell it from the Hulk's point of view.

Imagine he's this huge, strong, muscle-bound guy who has to stay angry, because if he calms down he'll turn into Bill Bixby.

Poor bastard!

Discuss your ideas with people who care. Few things are more tiresome than hypothetical conversations about a subject you don't like.

You two should have spent more time studying schoolwork and less time reading comics.

Then what would we have to talk about?

Your successful careers, maybe.

That'd be boring.

Yeah, not like this.

The first panel is a direct quote from a very loud conversation I heard Ric have with the cashier at a comic-book shop. The bit about the Hulk is all me.

Often, things will happen that call for a humorous comment, but are inherently difficult or offensive to joke about.

The harder you try to be funny, the less funny you'll be. Describe the situation bluntly and honestly, then simplify it.

Pop-culture references can help you describe complex situations by reminding people of a similar situation they already know and understand.

Not everyone will perceive things the way you will. Our jokes often tell more about us than our resumes can.

Windows Vista has a PR problem, partly due to a series of successful, hilarious ads that are inaccurate and insulting.

I'm a Mac.

And I'm a PC.

What's wrong, PC?

I'm impotent.

Recently Microsoft has countered with a series of ads of their own. Ads that are inconsistent in quality.

I'm a human being, not a human doing, a human being ...

... paid to be in this ad.

A better approach would be to find a trustworthy, telegenic Vista user to list the advantages of Windows Vista.

I have personally been using Vista for over a year. I find it to be a huge improvement over XP. It has given me no problems.

More than one company makes Windows PCs, providing a greater variety of hardware options and substantially lower prices.

Windows' 80% market share ensures easy availability of great software.

And, unlike Apple, the short-tempered megalomaniac who founded Microsoft has retired.

Then sum it up with a pithy slogan that'll stay in people's memory.

Microsoft®

IN CASE YOU HADN'T NOTICED WE'VE ALREADY WON

How to Face Your Fear

We all have things that terrify us. It's important to get them out in the open. Keeping them secret just gives them more power.

Birds. I'm terrified of birds.

Like hawks and vultures?

Yes.

That's certainly understandable.

And pigeons.

Oh.

And Big Bird. The way his right arm just hangs there. God, it's creepy!

Fear is seldom rational, so others might not understand your fears without explanation.

It's their sharp little beaks and talons. It's like they're designed to pluck out my eyeballs and eat them like grapes.

You're being silly.

I am?

Yeah! I doubt birds even eat grapes.

As I've said before, knowledge is fear's enemy. Learn as much as possible about that which you fear.

Effortlessly, the trained hornbill swoops in for the catch when his trainer throws a grape into the air.

I stand corrected.

Greater knowledge will lead to greater understanding, which will usually lead to less fear.

Hunting and deforestation have endangered many of these beautiful, irreplaceable creatures.

They don't seem so scary now, do they?

No, clearly we have the tools to defeat them!

That's not ... eh, that'll do.

I wrote this one after seeing a show at Disney's Animal Kingdom called Flights of Wonder. The show can be described as "birds of prey swooping at your head."

63

How to Keep Your Job in Perspective

No matter how bad your job is, there are jobs out there that are worse.

> Do you like working here?
>
> Could be worse. I could be a rodeo clown.
>
> You think about this a lot, don't you?
>
> Every single day.

Pick any job and you'll be able to find enough hardship in it that you'll be grateful to have your job.

> Rodeo clowns put on a clown suit and distract a bull that a bull rider got mad so the rider can get away unharmed to date big-haired hick women who wouldn't give a rodeo clown the time of day.
>
> Also, their workplace smells like manure.
>
> There's that too.

Focus on the work, not how you feel about the work. Distract yourself from your work, with your work.

> Well, you need to put on a suit. An angry client's coming in later and you're going to have to take his complaint, because I'm getting outta here.
>
> I have a date.
>
> YES SIR!

The ability to keep your job in proper perspective is a vital coping skill. You will likely use it every day you work.

> This is my date, Darla.
>
> Pleased to meet you.
>
> Whatever.
>
> Yup, at least I'm not a rodeo clown.
>
> That'd suck!

Wow, that's one jacked-up drawing of a big-haired hick woman! Luckily, the more distorted a drawing of a woman is, the more likely she seems to date Mullet Boss.

Even the best jokes get taken seriously, which is often painfully awkward.

What'd the boss wanna talk to you about?

Ponies and boys, mostly.

Why?

Because ... they're ... dreamy.

Build on the joke, making it more and more outlandish until it's obvious that you must be joking.

He likes them with a golden, flowing mane and a fiery temper.

I didn't realize he was that into ponies.

Actually, I'm talking about the boys.

If that fails, admit that you're joking. It's unpleasant, but letting the joke get out of hand will be even worse.

I was just kidding.

You don't hafta lie. If pretending to share the boss's "eccentricities" are what you have to do to get ahead in this place, I understand.

But I'm not lying.

And I'm not getting ahead.

If they still don't get the joke, let it go. The fact that they don't get it can be an effective joke in its own right.

Jenkins's desk is covered with pictures of ponies and copies of "Tiger Beat." Would you keep an eye on him?

Sure, it should be good for a laugh.

I'm not sure it's funny.

I am.

This strip contains an homage to a comedian buddy, Dennis Mitchell. He used to "take a break" during his act. He'd light a cigarette and read "Tiger Beat."

65

There are movies people expect you to have seen. If you haven't seen one of these films, people won't accept it.

You haven't seen "Beauty and the Beast"?!

Why would I?

It has violence and monsters and a guy with fire for hands.

That does sound like my kind of movie.

When watching the movie, show some enthusiasm. Demonstrate that you're giving the movie a fair chance.

Yeah, that's right! Go kick some @$$!

I keep telling you, Gaston's not the hero!

It seems the villagers disagree.

People seldom love movies for rational reasons, so try to avoid being too analytical and dissecting the movie.

So, he takes her captive and eventually she falls in love with him.

Yes, isn't it romantic?

No. It's Stockholm Syndrome.

Even if you don't enjoy the movie, try to enjoy the fact that the person sharing the movie enjoys it.

I really identify with Belle.

Of course you do. She's the world's prettiest nerd.

And she's in love with a foul, hairy monster.

Well, any analogy breaks down if you push it too far.

The most tragic part of "Beauty and the Beast" is that even after he has turned back into a good-looking man, everyone still seems to call him "Beast."

How to Get Vindication

We all have stories from our pasts that are unbelievable. Especially those of us that grew up on farms.

When I was a kid, a guy came to our farm and castrated our sheep for a case of beer.

So?

He did it with his teeth.

I assume he drank the beer first.

If you tell unbelievable stories, sooner or later someone will doubt you. That's why they're called "unbelievable."

Why would anyone do that?

He said that it was faster and cheaper than buying a lot of special equipment.

But can you put a price on dignity?

Yes. A case of beer.

Bide your time. If it's really that important, sooner or later you will find a way to prove that you weren't lying.

Tonight on "Dirty Jobs," Mike helps castrate sheep.

WHY ARE YOU DOING IT WITH YOUR TEETH?!

It's cheaper and faster.

I'd hoped.

And you thought I was lying!

Once you have been proved honest, take a moment to enjoy the rare sensation of vindication.

I suppose you're feeling pretty good about yourself.

Would you?

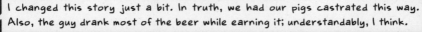

I changed this story just a bit. In truth, we had our pigs castrated this way. Also, the guy drank most of the beer while earning it; understandably, I think.

How to Stay Young

We're all getting older, but occasionally you notice that you're getting older.

> Working night-vision goggles being sold as a toy for $60! Things've changed.

> Why are you looking for night-vision goggles? That's kinda weird.

> I'm not. I'm looking at toys.

> Also weird.

As unsettling as it is to notice that you're getting older, it's even worse when someone else notices.

> When I was a kid we didn't have this stuff!

> Yeah! When you were a kid you played with sticks!

> I'll tell you what else, when I was a kid my mom didn't make fun of my dad

> Yeah, she divorced him.

> Good point.

In a sense, you're only as old as you feel, so don't be afraid to take steps to make yourself feel younger.

> Hey baby, good news!

> Good news would be that you didn't spend $60 on a toy meant for twelve-year-old kids.

> Indeed! It was marked for ages ten and up!

Don't overdo it, though. Trying too hard to seem young is creepy and unseemly.

> What are you doing?

> JUST TURN ON THE LAMP!

> Reading in the dark! Isn't it awesome?!

> The light would keep you from sleeping.

> Knowing you're sitting there wearing night-vision goggles won't help me sleep either.

Working "toy" night-vision goggles. Kinda makes me angry at kids. They have this stuff and I didn't. I won't act on it though. They have superior weapons.

Sometimes we all wake up in a good mood. We don't know when it will happen, but we're glad when it does.

If you are in a good mood, keep quiet about it. Others may not share your mood and won't want to hear about it.

Unhappy people may unload on you, like a drowning man pushing a lifeguard underwater to raise themselves up.

If they try this, use their bad mood to make your mood better, like a lifeguard drowning the jerk pushing them down.

One way to talk without really saying anything is to talk solely about subjects the listener doesn't care about.

> I found this great cable channel. It's all about hiking and camping and fishing.

> Is it called "The Stuff Scott Avoids Channel"?

> It's called "Outdoor Life Network."

> So, pretty much yes.

Another method is to hold forth at length on a subject about which your knowledge is incomplete at best.

> There was a show about two guys hiking.

> Where?

> Dunno. Anyway, they had this thing they drank out of to make the water safe to drink.

> What does it remove from the water?

> Stuff.

> No one wants stuff in their water.

You can also tell long, rambling stories that have no discernible point at all.

> So, two guys somewhere didn't drink "stuff" out of a "thing." What was this show called?

> I didn't catch the title.

> Well thanks for sharing.

> It was my pleasure.

> Yes, it was.

If all else fails, state obvious facts that everyone else already knows as if they are your own profound discoveries.

> This is how you all feel when I talk about science fiction, isn't it?

> And video games.

> And you all just listen politely.

> Yup.

> So ... tell me more about the thing.

> It had, like, a doohickey on it!

Another technique I've seen is replacing parts of the story's dialogue with "Dadadada." Which is like saying, "I know this isn't important, but I'll keep talking."

A reaction that releases a tremendous amount of energy can start with one lone particle (or poorly chosen word).

I yelled at my kids last night.

That's gotta be hard.

You know it.

Being a parent seems like the world's toughest hobby.

And I thought I was done yelling.

Once the reaction has begun, it can be slowed by inserting a carbon rod (or apology) to absorb the energy.

I'm sorry I said that parenting is a hobby.

You should be sorry!

And I am.

Sorry.

That I said it.

Out loud.

In your presence.

If you are to sustain the reaction, you must find a balance that absorbs excess energy without stopping the reaction.

Parenting is a difficult and vital task.

Thank you.

But it's not a career. Nobody pays you to do it.

YOU STUPID

And childbirth is a miracle.

Well, of course.

The only miracle people can perform by accident.

It's vital to note that if the reaction should get out of hand, the results would be thoroughly devastating.

The women in your office have declared you an outcast, you idiot.

So?

So, dummy, they'll shun anyone who talks to you. I'm only allowed to talk to you if I insult you at least once in every sentence I say ... you moron.

You already do that.

I know what the ladies like, and it ain't you.

Some people feel the need to stand uncomfortably close to you when they talk. This is, by definition, unpleasant.

There may be a logical reason for their proximity. Remain calm and ask them why they are standing so close to you.

Even if there is a good reason, spare yourself unnecessary discomfort by getting the conversation over quickly.

You always have the right to tell them to back off and give you some room. You are not the one being rude.

In case you didn't grow up in America, a "Wet Willy" is when you lick your finger and stick it in someone's ear. It's not sexual; try it on your spouse and see!

The first step in the breaking-in process for modern electronics is to savor the unpacking of your cool new device.

Once it's unpacked, familiarize yourself with the operation of the new gadget.

Use the gadget every chance you get. This will be fun, and it will help you find its strengths and weaknesses.

Sadly, you'll know you're accustomed to your new gadget when you start considering upgrading or replacing it.

With families spread out all over the country, many of us have to buy gifts for people we really don't know.

Don't hesitate to ask someone who knows the recipient better what they might like. How else will you find out?

After the gift has been received, you should contact your informant again to see if the recipient enjoyed the gift.

If they didn't like the gift, next time you can go another direction. If they liked it, get them something similar.

The first step to revealing the killer's identity is, of course, to figure out who the killer is.

Gather all of the suspects together in one room. Address them in a calm, refined, dignified manner.

One by one, recount each suspect's motives for committing the crime.

Then, with a theatrical flourish, reveal the killer's identity. Be prepared, for he will almost certainly deny it.

 When I was six my house was burglarized. One item they took was my dad's Sherlock Holmes pipe, like the one in panel two. Stupid smart-aleck burglars.

My words are my most valuable asset. Indeed, what most people think is my personality is often just my vocabulary.

Sometimes there is a situation that doesn't justify a lie, but the truth is out of the question. Words can help.

The more words you know, the more choices you have, and choosing the right word can make a big difference.

It may seem pointless to know several words that mean the same thing, but subtlety is always worth the trouble.

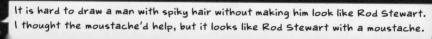

It is hard to draw a man with spiky hair without making him look like Rod Stewart. I thought the moustache'd help, but it looks like Rod Stewart with a moustache.

76

People tend to glide through their lives without thinking about who they really are until an event makes it obvious.

Of course!

Did you TiVo "Tron"?

Why?

Because it's bitchin'! Is that uncool?

Not as uncool as using the word "bitchin'."

Often it's not your behavior that will make you see who you are, so much as others' reactions to your behavior.

I never realized you were a hard-core "Tron" fan.

We prefer to be called "Tronnies."

REALLY?! You prefer "Tronnies"? What's that short for, "TRONsexuals"? "TRONsvestites"?!

That's what you call people who dress up in Tron costumes.

Once you've had a glimpse of your true self, it's time for introspective testing of your personal limits.

Are you gonna buy a Tron costume?

No, the ones you buy suck. To get a good one, you have to make it yourself.

Wow. I'm glad you're lazy.

Yeah, think about that next time you want me to do the dishes.

Odds are you won't have a rational explanation for why you are who you are. People who love you shouldn't ask.

But it's a terrible movie!

I love it despite its shortcomings. Can you understand that?

Yes. I can.

Good ideas are rare, so having one and then forgetting it is maddening.

I had a good idea earlier, but I can't remember it now.

It would have been a good idea to write it down, but I guess two good ideas a day would be too much to hope for.

So it would seem.

One way to prevent idea loss is to take notes. Unfortunately notes are often written in a hurry, and are inconsistent.

I did write a note, but it isn't helpful.

What's it say?

Uh, never mind. I don't wanna talk about it.

The note says "remember idea," doesn't it?

Shut up.

Another method is to tell your idea to someone else in hopes that they'll be able to remember it later if you can't.

If it was a good idea I must've told you. Are you sure you don't remember?

Yes, I'm sure I don't remember you saying anything that sounded like a good idea.

As a last resort, think about what you were doing when you had the idea. Try to recapture your train of thought.

It was an idea for the comic. How to ... hmm.

You were reading me one of your poems ... YES!!

I said it gave me an idea for a comic. "How to Quell Stupefying Boredom"!! Remember that?!

Now that you mention it, that does sound familiar

Sometimes we are made to perform mindless, repetitive tasks. Luckily, there's often technology that can help.

I've decided to go digital.

GOOD FOR YOU! It's about time.

Yeah, well, it always seemed like so much trouble, then I realized I could make you do it.

Here's my address book. Get cracking.

Often some preparation will be involved in making the task suitable for computerized processing methods.

What are you doing?

Cutting the pages out of the boss's address book so I can scan them faster.

Wouldn't it be simpler to just enter it manually?

Yes, but this way I get to destroy something of his.

Can I help?

And bear in mind that no technology is perfect. You will need to check the results for quality and accuracy.

How's it going?

The character-recognition program can't read his handwriting. I'm having to hand correct all of it.

That's pointless. You're just typing it all out after all.

No, I'm deleting it, THEN I'm retyping it.

Awesome.

At the end of the day you'll enjoy the satisfaction that comes from having worked smarter, rather than harder.

I saved your addresses to a file on your hard drive.

Great!

You're gonna ask me how to print the whole thing out, aren't you.

No. I'm going to tell you to print it out.

How silly of me.

Rereading this comic now, I feel like I should send Scott Adams a royalty. At least my boss doesn't have pointy hair. He has a mullet. There's a big difference.

When you are engaged in competition, it's important that you take it seriously.

Mental preparation techniques such as pep talks, visualizations, and positive thinking can be very helpful.

When the competition begins, you must clear your mind of all distractions and focus solely on the challenge at hand.

No matter what the outcome, be gracious. If you lose, don't make excuses and if you win, don't gloat.

 I came up with the "Walk like an Egyptian" joke and spent a year waiting for a comic it'd fit into. Another thing, Electronic Battleship is a waste of batteries.

They say there are three ghosts, but it's actually four. The first introduces the others, an "MC ghost," if you will.

Ghost number two, AKA "The First Ghost," will show you your past in an effort to demonstrate your potential.

The next ghost shows you the present from a new perspective to illustrate the repercussions of your actions.

The last ghost will warn of the terrible fate you'll suffer unless you take action to correct your many mistakes.

One of our mutual friends calls Ric "MC Ghost" because of this strip. If you think I'm too cruel to Ric, reflect on the fact that our friends side with me.

In Monopoly, victory is usually decisive and protracted, which can be terribly demoralizing for those who do not win.

Remind your opponent that there is a substantial amount of luck in the game. As such, losing is not his fault.

Be careful not to gloat. You want to act as if you're enjoying the game, not your friend's failure and humiliation.

Worse than gloating is to present false hope that your opponent may yet win. This can be patronizing and even cruel.

Running gags are funny mainly because they continue for so long. They usually start with a joke that isn't very good.

Instead of letting the joke die, build on it to make it funnier and keep it alive.

Keep at it long after those around you find it funny. The more you irritate others, the more you'll enjoy it.

Then let it fade away. After time has passed, dredge the joke up and it will be far funnier than it ever was before.

*I have read my comments page, and in an effort to make my wife look more "feminine" and less "like a lesbian," I've replaced her image with drawings of the beautiful actress Portia de Rossi

Start by getting the advice of your friends. They know and can point out your strengths and weaknesses.

I've got an interview for a better job. Any advice?

Yes. Get the job! Your job blows.

Any advice on how to get the job?

I can't give you all the answers.

If your clothes seem disheveled and poorly coordinated, so will you. Be sure to wear your finest clothes.

That's quite an outfit.

Thank you. I agree.

Strike a delicate balance. You need to seem to want the job, but you don't want to seem to need the job.

Are you interested in the position?

Indeed! To some extent.

Is the pay adequate?

Yes, I suppose.

Do you even know what the job is?

Of course! I think.

Often you'll be asked what can only be called "a BS question." You have no choice but to fight BS with BS!

What would you say is your greatest shortcoming as an employee?

I'm so super-competent that other people tend to treat me with suspicion and hostility.

I find that doubtful.

See?

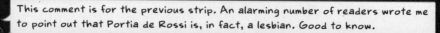

This comment is for the previous strip. An alarming number of readers wrote me to point out that Portia de Rossi is, in fact, a lesbian. Good to know.

84

It's only a matter of time. Sooner or later, the Moon-Men will invade, and we can't afford to be caught off guard.

PITIFUL EARTH-MEN!!

We're here to free your planet ... from you. We tire of watching you squander your greatest resource.

GRAVITY!

Of course, we do have gravity on the moon, just not as much of it. THE DETAILS ARE UNIMPORTANT!!

The army will be useless, but one man utilizing technology developed in secret can surprise and confuse the enemy.

Emperor, our forces are being decimated by a single man who is wearing some manner of rocket-propelled hat.

CURSE THOSE DEVIOUS EARTH-MEN!!

This doesn't mean it will be easy. Odds are, you will be captured, and will seem utterly defeated and helpless.

Now you see the folly of resisting the will of the Moon-Men.

Your planet will soon be ours, and you'll be best man when I Moon-marry your girlfriend.

And you're helpless to prevent it, for we have cut your chin strap!

WA-HAHAHAHAHAHAHAHA hehehehe HAH!

But overconfidence will cause the Moon-Men to underestimate you, making their ultimate defeat all the more ironic.

The Earth-Man escaped! He's destroying our army!

BUT HOW!

He tied a knot in his chin strap. Ironically, it's only our lack of gravity that allows it to support his weight!

We don't lack gravity. Earth just has more ... THE DETAILS ARE NOT IMPORTANT!!

This is the first appearance of Rocket Hat and the Moon-Men. For more information about Moon-Men, turn to page 114, or check your local library!

Random facts, or "factoids," can be a good way to start a conversation.

Hello.

Did you know that Thomas Edison invented the word "hello"?

I bet Tesla invented a better word.

Yup. The government probably doesn't want us to know about it.

They can also be a good way to kill one.

Did you know that most birds don't have penises?

No. I didn't.

Well now you do.

Yes, and nothing can change that.

Just throwing out more factoids will not resuscitate a conversation that flat lined due to poor factoid use.

Ducks do have penises. It's really very interesting, you see ...

We'd rather not talk about duck penises.

Agreed.

Cats' penises have tiny little barbs on them.

In order for a factoid to spur discussion, it must be related to the topic at hand.

Did you know he has received over thirty rejection letters for his book, "Wild Wangs: Male Genitalia in the Animal Kingdom"?

How many restraining orders?

Just one, from the National Geographic Society.

The damned narrow-minded

A know-it-all is someone who constantly corrects you, even when you're right and they're wrong. Nobody enjoys that.

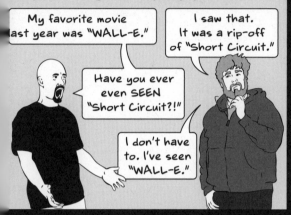

If you know you are right, you can try to shut them down with your superior knowledge. This plan never works.

Know-it-alls must contradict you. It's what they do. As such, you can steer the conversation in entertaining directions.

Or you can avoid them. One thing is for certain: confronting them about their behavior will be ineffective.

 The "WALL-E"/"Short Circuit" conversation is one I actually had. It's odd: I love science fiction, but conversations about it often end with me yelling.

I must start by stating in clear terms that I would never endorse alcohol to minors.

Nurse your drink as long as possible. People see that you have a drink in your hand whether it's a new drink or not.

Order your drinks with shock value in mind. Try to get people to focus on what you're drinking, rather than how much.

Now the most important part. All of the other directions hinge on this point. Be a lightweight. It saves time and money.

Comedians expect to be allowed to get drunk at work, and often get pissy if they are charged for their drinks. I got a lot of work just for being sober-ish.

Occasionally we all have experiences from which we'd like to flee but cannot, because we are being paid to stay put.

My client's angry.

I don't doubt it.

You're gonna go listen to his complaint.

Is that my job? "Abuse receptacle"?

I prefer to think that I buy your self-esteem and convert it into customer satisfaction.

Physically you're stuck, but in your imagination you can go to your favorite place, and be with your favorite people.

Ah, somewhere other than work. What could be better?

Being somewhere other than work with several hot supporting characters from various sci-fi TV series?

Good point!

Sadly, reality can often encroach on your fantasy with disturbing results.

It's time to have some kinda freaky space orgy.

I am in favor of that.

We know you're shiftless, so we'll do all the work.

Sounds good.

TAKE ME INCOMPETENTLY!

Whatever works for you, baby.

Even more disturbing, your fantasy can sometimes encroach on reality.

Whatever works for you, baby.

WHAT?! Did you just call me "baby"?

Wha ... uh, YES! Because you cry like a baby!

Oh. Good!

You don't mind me insulting you?

I mind it less than the alternative.

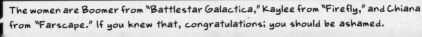

The women are Boomer from "Battlestar Galactica," Kaylee from "Firefly," and Chiana from "Farscape." If you knew that, congratulations; you should be ashamed.

89

We all fall back on old sayings to get us through life, despite the fact that they are often unhelpful at best.

I just can't get any traction with the ladies lately.

Well, you can't always get what you want.

That is true. For example, I wanted you to say something useful.

Examine the exact wording of the saying. Subtle word choices can imbue the saying with deeper layers of meaning.

Lemme finish. You can't always get what you want, but if you try sometimes, you might find you can get what you need.

"Might"?

So you could also say, "You can't always get what you want, but you might find you can't get what you need either."

Yes, but that's not as uplifting.

Look at who coined the saying and what the situation was at the time. Historical context leads to greater understanding.

And isn't that from a song by the Rolling Stones?

Well, yeah.

Those guys have always enjoyed an abundance of both what they want, and what they need.

I dunno. They all needed to get clean and sober.

Yeah, but they didn't want to.

Only by understanding the author and his intent can you truly understand the true meaning of a common, clichéd phrase.

I tell you my problems and you tell me that some British multimillionaire rock stars say that it may or may not all work out.

In a nutshell, yes.

Thank you. You've been very helpful.

Really?

Yes. You've taught me never to tell you my problems again.

First, let them tell you the problem. Stating it out loud will give them clarity and help avoid assumptions on your part.

I have a problem.

I'm glad to hear you finally admit it.

The good news is that there are products that can help with the odor.

What? SHUT UP! It's my daughter.

They make the same product for women. It's light blue ...

WILL YOU SHUT UP?!

Step out of your point of view and try to see the problem from their perspective.

She's thirteen and she signed up for a sport.

That's good! You want her to be active.

Wrestling.

Well, in this day and age, there's nothing wrong with girls participating in Coed wrestling.

Okay, yeah. That's a nightmare.

THANK YOU!!!

If you are unable to actually help your friend, suggest people who can and encourage your friend to seek them out.

What's your ex say about it? She's the girl's mother, after all. She must have an opinion.

She's all for it. Told her to go "kick some man butt."

Wow! I didn't expect that.

You weren't married to her.

If your friend chose to share their problem with you, they must think you can help, and you owe it to them to try.

Well, if she's going to be wrestling, that makes hygiene even more important.

So anyway, it's a light blue container that says "strong enough for a man."

I despise you.

Hey, I'm just the messenger.

I got many complaints. People thought I was saying girls are too weak to wrestle boys. Actually, I think boys are too weak to be trusted while wrestling girls.

Lying for recreational purposes can be very different from lying for professional purposes, which we all do every day.

In order for the lie to be fun, it must be so extreme that there is little chance of any sane person ever believing it.

The fun comes not from convincing someone that the lie is true, but rather in trying to make them disprove it.

Of course, if someone is dumb enough to believe you, that's a lot of fun too.

While it is rewarding to make repairs yourself, sometimes you will have an automotive problem you can't fix.

When talking to your mechanic, try to describe the problem as best you can.

Be patient. Try to remember that the diagnostic process is not an exact science, and can be frustrating.

Most mechanics are decent people trying to make a living. There are crooks out there, though, so be respectful but wary.

Wrote this one after my car window self-destructed. It got a lot of positive feedback from mechanics. Turns out they don't enjoy being treated like thieves! Go figure.

History is not often made without struggle. If you are to have a place in history, you must face adversity.

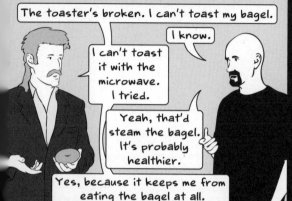

Also, history is not often made without luck. Keep your eyes open for any opportunities providence may send you.

History is never made by one man alone. Surround yourself with the best people and give them opportunities to excel.

History is not made in your lifetime. Future generations will decide if you are to be remembered, and for what.

How to Perform a Spoken-word Rendition of a Popular Song

Your spoken-word piece deserves an introduction that tells the audience they are about to see something significant.

When I asked Scott to participate in this talent show, I didn't think he'd say yes.

When he told me what he intended to do, I told him not to go to the trouble, but he did.

So I hope you get some enjoyment out of ... what's about to happen.

This is theater. Use costuming, props, and special camera techniques to set the appropriate world-weary, romantic tone.

Why'd you have to drag me into this?

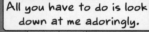

All you have to do is look down at me adoringly.

I'll do half of that.

Choose a song with multiple layers of meaning, and use your vocal skills to emphasize key words and phrases.

Close your eyesssss. Give ME your hand! Do you feel my HEART BEATING?! DO YOU understand? Do you FEEL the same?

AM I only dreaming? Or is this burning ... **AN ETERNAL FLAME?!**

Afterward, try to remain humble in the face of the adulation you receive, but make it clear you're proud of your work.

Wasn't that an old Bangles song?

I like to think I made it my own.

Well, I'm sure they don't want it back after what you did to it.

People assume I'm making fun of William Shatner, but I'm actually referencing Telly Savalas's rendition of "If." Look it up. It'll change your life, maybe for the better!

How to Drive a Long Distance

There are some trips you'll take that are too close for flying to be practical, but too far for driving to be fun.

We're driving to Spokane to meet with a vendor.

Why not have them come here?

I'd never ask someone else to make that trip.

But you're asking me to.

No, I'm telling you to. There's a difference.

The key to enjoying a long drive is to stay entertained, and the most effective entertainment is good company.

Then when I'm done with the pumice, I slather them with moisturizer.

I don't want to hear about your foot calluses!!

Then you shouldn't have asked.

I asked how you've been, over an hour ago. And you're right. I shouldn't have.

If you're driving alone, or your driving companion is asleep, a good audio book can make the miles melt away.

Al asked Dirk if he needed a doctor.

"No," Dirk replied, gritting his teeth. "I'll grind it down with a pumice stone, then I'll slather my foot with moisturizer."

For more information, ask the true experts on distance driving: long-haul truckers. They'll have plenty of advice.

NEVER pass a semi on the right!!

Anything else?

Yeah. After driving ten hours a day, six straight days, you go to a place where happiness cannot reach you, and you no longer care to live.

What do I do then?

Pass a semi on the right.

How to Make a Recommendation

Occasionally, one of your friends will be on the verge of a mistake and it will fall to you to help them avoid it.

I'm thinking of buying a used sofa.

That's a terrible idea. You have no idea what the previous owner might have done to that sofa.

No, but I know what I've done to my current sofa, and it needs to be replaced.

Recommend a positive course of action that you believe will lead to success.

You, my friend, need to go to IKEA.

What's an IKEA?

It's a cross between a huge, stylish furniture store with low prices and a gigantic baffling maze.

Like a corn maze with end tables?

Yes, but corn is spelled with a K and an umlaut.

It may take some convincing to get your friend to follow your recommendation.

So it's cheap furniture.

"Inexpensive." There's a difference.

Is the stuff well made?

That depends. You assemble it yourself.

So in your case, probably not.

Ask how the situation worked out. By intervening, you've earned a certain amount of credit or blame.

IKEA was awesome!

As always.

I bought a ton of stuff!

As always.

I really screwed up assembling my new sofa, though.

As always. You can just buy a new one in a few months.

I think we just discovered IKEA's business model.

Scandinavians aren't known for being dumb.

IKEA came to Orlando shortly after I did. Many people didn't know what it was. I discovered it's hard to explain without sounding insane. The names throw people.

How to Unify Newtonian Physics and Quantum Mechanics

First, develop a clear definition of the two theories you intend to unify.

Once that's done, define the problems that have prevented their unification.

Now drill down. The more detailed your analysis of the problem, the better the chance that you will find the solution.

Focus on areas of commonality between the theories. Finding how they are the same may show why they are different.

I know the title is vague, but think about it. Everybody has to ask "WHAT?!" from time to time.

Hey baby!

What?

Hmph.

Nothing.

No, seriously. What?!

Nothing. Drop it.

Drop what?

NOTHING!!

How do I drop "nothing"?

Just shut up about it!

WHAT?!

The answer to "WHAT?!" is usually something you did wrong. Try to find out what you did wrong, and to whom.

You're clearly mad. Are you mad at me?

What makes you think I'm mad?

Well, you're pouting.

Okay, I'm mad at you.

What for?

Accusing me of pouting, for one thing.

It's usually pretty easy to figure out who you've offended. Finding out how you offended them can be much harder.

But before that, what were you mad at me for?

What do you think?

Ah, now I have to list everything I've done wrong so you can confirm which error you're mad about.

Well played.

Thank you.

I'll start with "I'm too awesome."

Once you've decided who you angered and how, you'll have to decide if you owe them an apology. Odds are you do.

It doesn't matter what I did. Whatever it was clearly upset you, and I am sorry.

Aw. Thanks.

So what did I do?

It's not important.

Hmph.

What?!

I'm lucky. My wife doesn't actually play these kinds of games. If she's mad at me she tells me exactly, in great detail, why. Doesn't sound like a blessing, but it is.

Prepare your audience. Make sure they are aware that they are about to see something of great significance.

I have, beneath this sheet, something amazing.

Is it a pedestal?

No. It's a historical item that belonged to a great man.

Is it Lincoln's pedestal?

No. Shut up.

When the time comes to unveil the item, do so with flair. Instill your audience with the proper sense of awe and wonder.

Behold, Gandhi's gun!

And a pedestal.

SHUT UP!

Tell your audience the item's story as vividly as you can. Artifacts and stories can help make history come alive.

It's a silver-plated revolver with carved ivory handles that say, "The Passive Resister."

Gandhi wouldn't have owned a gun!

He certainly wouldn't have owned a fancy gun!

It was given to him as a gift by Truman. He didn't know Gandhi very well.

If your audience has any questions, answer them patiently and thoroughly.

Did you make this up?

No.

How'd you get it?

eBay.

Did the guy who sold the gun to you make this up?

I sincerely hope not.

I had an idea long ago about Superman buying a gun. Nobody else found it funny. I mean nobody! I then changed it beyond all recognizability (Cont'd on next page)

Comfort is subjective. An uncomfortable temperature for others may not bother you. Which will bug them even more.

Where's your coat?

Don't need one.

Aren't you freezing?

Nope.

So you're not bothered at all by the cold.

That depends. By "the cold" do you mean the temperature, or the people who are cold?

Confused by your lack of discomfort, cold people will demand an explanation, but no explanation will satisfy them.

Why aren't you shivering?

Maybe I'm just tougher than you.

HA!

That wasn't a joke.

I know. That's why it was funny.

The best strategy is to give them an explanation that'll kill the conversation and hopefully make them go away.

I'm sick and have a fever.

It's contagious.

Hiiiiiiiiiighly contagious.

I gotta go.

Riiiiiiiiiiiight.

Be patient with them and take heart, because come summer, chances are your roles will be reversed.

I'm sick and have chills.

It's contagious.

Hiiiii

Never mind. Point taken.

I'm sorry. It's just that I'm so miserably hot.

HA!

That wasn't a joke.

I know. We've been through this before.

into a piece about Gandhi's gun in an effort to make it funny to other people. The general consensus was that "Lincoln's pedestal" is much funnier.

Many of man's celebratory rituals are inherently embarrassing. None more so than the dreaded "high-five."

As with other detestable habits, people will attempt to get you to join in their folly with peer pressure and coercion.

If you must participate in a "high-five," take care to do it right. If you're gonna do the wrong thing, at least do it right.

Prevent the "high-five" from escalating to an "on the side" or a "down low" by gripping their hand and shaking it.

The only guys who like to "high-five" are ones who look cool doing it, or think that they do. I don't believe anyone looks cool "high-ing five," so do the math.

If you enjoy a movie, you'll want to talk about it. Try not to discuss it too much with people who haven't seen it yet.

Have you seen "Watchmen" yet?

No.

Did you read the book?

No.

You should!

If I do, will you want to discuss it?

At length!

hen I promise, I will never see or read "Watchmen."

Instead, I suggest that you vote with your dollars by buying and displaying tie-in merchandise. Moderation is crucial.

Did you buy a "Watchmen" T-shirt? You could use a second T-shirt.

I got something much better!

It's kinda like my rubber Hulk fists.

The ones I told you to never wear in public?

And especially never while driving. Yeah, those are the ones.

The displayed merchandise will act as a conversation starter, instantly drawing in those who share your enthusiasm.

Wow, that qualifies as "something."

Yeah, It's like Dr. Manhattan

Dr. Manhattan. I get it. That's just wrong, man.

Well, it's too bright in here. In the dark you can see that it glows blue.

Oh, AWESOME!

CENSORED

It might also pique the interest of those who haven't seen the film, allowing you to converse with new, different people.

I can't wait for the guys at the precinct to see this!

Would you like to take a photo?

That won't be necessary.

CENSORED
CENSORED
ED

I'm told in Europe, Dr. Manhattan's man junk wasn't such a big deal. In America it was all we could talk about. Clearly, this is because of our moral superiority.

Today's kids weren't there to see the relative deprivation of your youth. The only way they'll know is if you tell them.

You kids these days are so incredibly lucky!

Really? Why?

Were adults even more irritating and self-righteous when you were young?

Of course, telling them, even in great detail, doesn't guarantee that they'll understand what you're trying to say.

At my school, the playground equipment was all made out of plumbing fixtures and sewer pipes coated with lead-based paint.

But you had a playground, so you were lucky, right?

You're missing the point.

Which is?

That you are ungrateful.

Try to use examples the kid can relate to, and details that will make your stories seem more real to them.

And your video games are so much better! I had a game where two blocky tanks shot square bullets at each other on a blank screen. If a tank got hit, it'd spin around and make a noise that kinda sounded like a fart.

That sounds kinda cool!

Okay, yeah. That was pretty cool.

Telling kids about the past will give them greater perspective, and the act of telling them may give you some as well.

Suffering made us tough, so we could grow up and make a better world for the next generation.

And then resent us for it.

Yes. Just like our parents did with us.

The game I mention is, of course, "Combat" for the Atari. Many Atari games rewarded young boys with a fart noise when they won. Atari knew its audience.

104

How to Live with a Disturbing Memory

Disturbing memories usually spring from disturbing events. We all experience them, and they can happen at any time.

As the disturbing thing happens, remain calm. Panicking would only make the experience even more memorable.

You'll be tempted to try to put the memory out of your mind. This never works, and leads to erratic behavior.

The only way to deal with the memory is to talk about it. Deal with your feelings in an honest and healthy manner.

How to Write Your Own Vows

Writing your own vows is a great way to make your wedding more personal and more nerve wracking.

My fiancée and I are writing our own vows.

My wife and I wrote each other's vows.

Really? How'd that work out?

I'm stuck doing all the dishes, but if I ask her, "Who runs Bartertown?" she has to say "Master Blaster."

Your vows should be romantic, and should give your guests a window into your intimate feelings.

I was thinking of starting like this.

I wasn't really a man before I met you.

That's nice.

Specifically, it was our second date when you made a man out of me.

That part needs work.

If you are unaccustomed to writing or public speaking, feel free to seek the opinions of a trusted friend.

Repeatedly and eagerly, despite the massive amount of booze flowing through our bodies ...

You do realize that her parents are gonna be there when you say this?

Yeah, that's why I lied and said it was the second date.

But don't let them exert too much influence on you. These are your vows, and they should reflect your feelings.

You should promise to be fair to her in the divorce.

No.

You're promising to be unfair to her? That's honesty!

I will not talk about divorce in my wedding vows!

So you're just gonna spring it on her in five to seven years. That's cold blooded, man.

I'll let you in on an inside joke. When I told Ric I was marrying Missy, he said, "I'm sure you'll have a lovely five to seven years together." It's been 13 years so far.

In this life, conflict is unavoidable. Your behavior before a fight is often just as important as your conduct during it.

THE ONLY CIVILIZED WAY TO SETTLE THIS DISPUTE IS TO FIGHT IT OUT!!

Choose your preferred method of combat.

I choose VIOLENCE!!

Very well. A VIOLENCE FIGHT IT SHALL BE!!

Regaling your adversary with vague threats will make them uncertain, or fill them with an ill-defined sense of doom.

IT IS GO TIME! FOR YOU!! And DOWN is the direction you will be GOING!!

Indeed, but I'll only be going to visit you, whom I will have sent down first.

You win this round.

Specific threats, on the other hand, will cause them to imagine the punishment they're about to receive in vivid detail.

I must warn you that I've developed my own unbeatable style of karate, which I've named "Fosse fu"!

That doesn't really sound menacing.

You'll change your mind after I've slapped you into submission with my jazz hands ...

... of fury!!

Be aware that eventually the time for talk will be over, and you will have to follow through on your threats.

Well, it's been three hours. Frankly, I don't see any violence happening. I propose a hot-wing duel. He who eats the hottest wing is the victor.

Loser pays for the wings?

Agreed. What were we fighting about anyway?

Whose turn it is to pay for hot wings.

Then it is settled!

The beauty of combat by jazz hands is that it makes fighting too undignified to even contemplate. It's a defense concept I call "Mutual Assured Humiliation."

We have discussed how to share a shocking truth already, but how you react to hearing one is far more telling.

Are you ready to receive the truth?

I'd like to think so.

'Cause I'm about to drop a truth load!

I'd like to change my answer.

It's too late. The truth load's already on deck!

When someone's telling you a shocking truth, try to listen with an open mind.

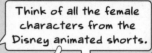

Think of all the female characters from the Disney animated shorts.

Minnie. Daisy. Clarabelle. That pig whose teats Mickey played like some kinda freaky xylophone.

Okay.

The truth is that not one of them was nearly as hot as Bugs Bunny in drag!

If the truth you are being told is in fact shocking, your mind will naturally rebel.

GHAAH!!!! I HATE YOU! I HATE YOU! I HATE YOU!

But do you disagree?

NO! That's why I hate you!!

I HATE YOU! I HATE YOU! I HATE YOU!

Once you've accepted the new truth, you will have to decide if you will share it further and risk the consequences.

Oh yeah, Bugs made a totally hot female! You know, I once made out with a chick in a Bugs Bunny costume!

SHUT UP!! I DON'T WANNA HEAR THIS!!

Fine.

Which of you was in the costume?

Both of us. It was a big costu

SHUT UP!!

 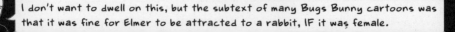
I don't want to dwell on this, but the subtext of many Bugs Bunny cartoons was that it was fine for Elmer to be attracted to a rabbit, IF it was female.

There are as many approaches to saving the Earth as there are people, and like people, most of them won't work.

Nice shirt.

I'm kind of an Earth Father.

In that I care about the Earth, but I'm too busy with my career to really put much effort into it.

EARTH MOTHER

Examine each approach critically, deciding which ones have a chance of achieving the desired goal.

We all have to follow the three Rs. Reduce. Reuse. Recycle.

Why?

So there'll be resources left for the next generation.

So you want to save the Earth, for YOUR KIDS.

Isn't that what's really important?

Not to the Earth.

EARTH MOTHER

Once you've found what you think is the right approach, share it with others.

So you're saying the faster mankind goes extinct, the better off the Earth will be.

Yup! The key is to follow what I call the three Ds.

Despoil. Dispose. Die out.

I think I may be ill.

That's a good start!

EARTH MOTHER

It may seem like a hopelessly large task, but you can make a lasting difference.

To get the word out, we're having the three Ds printed on ten thousand Styrofoam cups!

Those cups'll take centuries to degrade!

That's the idea!! Long after we've all died, they will be a lasting monument to our selflessness.

Are your names printed on them?

No, but yours is. As a thank-you for inspiring us!

EARTH MOTHER

For the first time in history, Mullet Boss and I are united against one common enemy. Fitting that the enemy is the environment we depend on to survive.

109

Seattle Weekly: Dining Issue

The first person in the traditional newspaper industry to give me the time of day was Mark Fefer, the editor of *Seattle Weekly*. He read my sample comics, met with me, made me a generous offer to run my comic in his paper and promoted it on the front page of the first issue in which it ran.

I thanked him by immediately moving across the continent.

A few months later, he called me and asked if I'd be interested in doing some comics for the yearly dining issue. Every year *Seattle Weekly* selects various categories of restaurant, (Best Place to Take a Date, Best Place to Broaden your Horizons) and picks the local restaurants that best fit those categories. Mark wanted me to create comics for the headers of each of the categories. It sounded like a very difficult assignment, but I felt bad about moving away so abruptly, and he was offering money, which always helps. What followed was two months obsessively trying to think of something funny to write about dining with kids, or tourists, or a hangover. Or possibly all three.

In the next few pages you'll find the best of what I produced. These comics have never appeared on my site, and only ran once in *Seattle Weekly*.

Enjoy.

Where to Conduct an Affair

Where to Go for a Romantic Date

Where to Take a First Date When You're Broke

Where to Eat When You're Bombed

Where to Hold Your Weekly Brunch Club

Where to Burn Your Mouth Off

Where to Dine and Drive

Where to Eat with Your Eyes

Where to Satisfy Your Ethics

Where to Meet Your Fellow Diners

Where to Go on a Date with Your Spouse

Where to Cure Your Hangover

Where to Have a Once-a-Year Splurge

Nah, I shouldn't.

Come on. We only do this once a year! You should treat yourself.

Darn it, you're right! I'm gonna have the steak fries!

Where to Get Kid-Friendly Food that You'll Enjoy Too

Today's special is beef filet, caked in cracked peppercorns and drizzled with a cream glaze.

Mmmm, that sounds lovely.

Shaped like a dinosaur.

YAY!!!

Where to Bring Tourists (Approved Version)

The soup here is just the best.

Dear, you didn't need to take us to the fanciest place in town. We'd be happy eating anywhere as long as we're with you.

Aw, that's sweet.

So, do you have a boyfriend?

The pie is also great!

Where to Bring Tourists (Original Version)

They don't have anything like this in Yakima.

What, themed restaurants?

Cloth napkins.

The "Where to Bring Tourists" strip on the left is the one that ran. It was felt that the original version betrayed a bit too much of my opinion of where I'm from.

Rocket Hat

In December of 2008, cartoonist Ray Friesen contacted me about collaborating on a project. He had been reading my back comics and thought a good graphic novel could be made from an idea I threw out in one of my comics. The idea was "Hard Day's Knight," in which England is threatened by an ancient evil, and the only way to save the country is to send in the Knights of the Realm, who nowadays are all aging actors and rock stars.

I agreed that it was a good idea for a story. Sadly, so did the guy who had recently sold a very similar idea to Dreamworks. Also in agreement was the guy who was suing him for plagiarism.

Ray and I started casting around for another idea to collaborate on, and settled on Rocket Hat vs. the Moon-Men. The plan was this: Ray would write a brief prologue, then I would write and draw the first installment of the story. It would be written in a style slightly sillier than *Basic Instructions*. I decided on my own to draw it in a cartoonier style, so that it would better match Ray's style. Ray is a far superior artist to me, and the idea of him trying to match what I refer to as my "art" was just distasteful to me.

When I finished, I'd send my work to Ray. He would pick up the story where I left off. He'd send his installment to me and we'd alternate until the story was done. The only rule was that each installment had to end in some kind of cliffhanger.

On the next two pages, you will find the first and only installment of *Rocket Hat* I produced, along with commentary and the reasons why we abandoned the project.

THE BEGINNING OF THE END ... OF THE BEGINNING!

WRITTEN AND DRAWN (IF YOU WANT TO CALL IT THAT) BY SCOTT MEYER

THE PROBLEMS BEGAN AS THEY OFTEN DO, WITH FULL MEDIA COVERAGE.

We interrupt soap operas for a breaking news bulletin!

GOOD!

BREAKING NEWS

THE GRATITUDE WAS SHORT LIVED.

Earth has received a threatening transmission. Analysts say there's reason to believe it may have emanated from the moon. We now play it in its entirety.

ATTENTION! This broadcast emanates from the moon!

We're here to free your planet ... from you! We tire of watching you squander your greatest resource.

GRAVITY!

This seems familiar somehow.

Of course, we do have gravity on the moon, just not as much of it. THE DETAILS ARE UNIMPORTANT!!

THE WHOLE WORLD WATCHED THE TRANSMISSION, TRANSFIXED IN TERROR.

And we want our rocks back too!

All of them.

THE MESSAGE WAS IMMEDIATELY FOLLOWED BY A PRESS CONFERENCE WITH THE VICE KING OF SPACE AMERICA.

There is nothing to worry about. The moon men will be powerless against the might of the Galactic Space Navy!

On an unrelated note, if anybody is in possession of any moon rocks, please call the government pronto!

ONE HOUR LATER, COMMODORE CAPP, SUPREME COMMANDER OF THE GALACTIC SPACE NAVY, ADDRESSED HIS TROOPS.

The whole planet is depending on us to save them from this terrible alien threat.

You all know what that means.

We are well and truly doomed.

First and foremost, I remember not being happy with the art. In retrospect, I guess it wasn't too bad for a first attempt. I quite like the drawing of Mullet Boss as vice king.

Ray gave Mullet Boss the title of vice king. If we'd kept going I planned to explain that he was king of the northern hemisphere, while someone else was king of the southern hemisphere. The Earth's logo (which you can see a bit of in panel five) is the Earth, divided in half on a field of red so that it inadvertently forms a kind of Ghostbusters symbol, but with the Earth in it instead of a ghost.

The moon rocks were going to come into play when the vice king tried to appease the Moon-Men by giving them all of their rocks back in a grand diplomatic ceremony. After receiving their rocks, the emperor of the moon and his Moon-Men would throw the rocks at any earthlings in range to demonstrate their continued hostility.

The name Commodore Capp is not an attempt at a joke about his love of hats. I was scrambling for a name and my eyes fell on a painting I own by my good friend Mike Capp. The similarity between the commodore and Captain Crunch was going to be explained later on. All high-ranking officials of the Galactic Space Navy are required to cultivate the Captain Crunch look as part of their uniform.

The design of the "Unbreakable" and the "Nondescript" was done entirely by Ray, and I think he did a fine job of it. My drawing of his design really doesn't do it justice.

The character Kirk Charles is named after a good friend of mine — a friend named Kirk Charles. He has led the most bizarre life of any human I know. I've tried to get him to write about it for my blog, but he never gets around to it. He has written porn for the mob. He has worked as a famous sex symbol's "personal undresser." He's a published authority on card marking. He briefly lived under an assumed name against his will. The assumed name was "Adrian." He has at different times, through no effort of his own, possessed a large collection of sex toys that had belonged to dead people, and the largest known collection of writings by and memorabilia about the poet Don Blanding.

He also procured for me a genuine Shriners' fez, which is quite a feat, as my understanding is that Shriners are supposed to be buried wearing them.

Back to *Rocket Hat*. In the end I realized that it'd take lots of time and effort to get my artwork up to a level that I could be proud of. I figured if I was going to put that much effort into a comic strip, it should probably be *Basic Instructions*.

The second installment of *Rocket Hat* (the first one by Ray) can be seen at: http://donteatanybugs.net/rockethat1.jpg

Thanx,
Scott Meyer

PART TWO OF THE END ... OF THE BEGINNING!
WRITTEN AND DRAWN (IF YOU WANT TO CALL IT THAT) BY SCOTT MEYER

WHEN WE LEFT OFF, THE SUPREME COMMANDER OF THE GALACTIC NAVY HAD CASUALLY MENTIONED THAT THE EARTH WAS DOOMED. FEW CIVILIANS WERE AWARE THAT THE GALACTIC SPACE NAVY CONSISTED OF TWO SHIPS.

The battle cruiser "Unbreakable."

UNBREAK-ABLE

And the space tug "Nondescript," which tows the "Unbreakable" everywhere it goes due to "Unbreakable"'s engines being irreparably broken.

THE SUPREME COMMANDER'S PRESS CONFERENCE CONTINUED.

We've gathered our greatest strategic minds, and their recommendation was to get everyone together and ask if anybody has any ideas.

Which we are doing, right now.

cough cough.

Anyone?

LUCKILY FOR EVERYONE, SITTING IN THE AUDIENCE WAS THE NAVY'S YOUNGEST REAR ADMIRAL, KIRK CHARLES. HE HAD RISEN TO HIS RANK BECAUSE HE POSSESSED THE ONE SKILL NAVIES OF ALL KIND, BE THEY OCEAN, SPACE OR GRAVY, PRIZED ABOVE ALL OTHERS.

HE WAS AN EXPERT HAT MAKER.

Come on, How about you?

You look smart.

AND SLOWLY BUT CONFIDENTLY, THIS HAT MAKER WAS RAISING HIS HAND.

WILL THE EARTH BE SAVED?
WHAT IS THE HAT MAKER'S IDEA?
IS THERE SOME HINT IN THE TITLE OF THE COMIC?
THE ANSWER TO AT LEAST ONE OF THESE QUESTIONS SHOULD BE YOURS IN THE NEXT INSTALLMENT OF ...

REAR ADMIRAL ROCKET HAT OF THE GALACTIC SPACE NAVY!!!

Afterword
By Ric Schrader

Assuming you are not the sort who jumps immediately to the afterword and thus have actually read this book, for you, it is already too late. You have already become enmeshed in the web of lies and deceit that is called "Basic Instructions."

Let me say that Meyer is my best friend, which makes this all the harder to write, for the Meyer that I knew, the simple, good-willed country boy with nothing in his heart other than the desire to make people happy, is long dead. Meyer has become a slave to his own horrible desires, more comic strip than man, twisted and cruel.

How did this come about? How did a man of such stalwart comedic values become such a figure-head of evil? Sadly, I do not know the answer. What I do know is that Meyer has become focused on the single-minded goal of destroying that which created him: the good, kindhearted folk of Sunnyside, Washington.

Sunnyside, as its name implies, is a pleasant, humble, Norman Rockwell–like town built on solid American beliefs, a town made of people who hew to the timeworn values of unending toil, har-vesting of corn and the slaughtering of cattle. Indeed, talk with Meyer even for a few minutes and you realize that, for him, in the end it all comes down to the slaughtering.

Many are the evenings that I have spent at Meyer's home (he, resplendent in his smoking jacket and Mexican wrestling mask), listening to his insane rants about the destruction of the good town and people of Sunnyside. For hours he will go on about his plans for the annihilation of this innocent burg, gesticulating wildly at a giant painting of the town he has created out of nubby plywood and pure evil and placed upended in a corner of his basement. His wild-eyed screeds, full of vitriol and retribution against a people that only sought to do him well, are broken only by the occasional ministrations of the latest in a series of Missys.

Yes, even Missy is, as you know her, a lie. Contrary to the widely-held belief that Missy is his longtime companion and devoted wife, the truth is that Missy has been nothing more than a string of beautiful playthings, a series of gorgeous women who have become enslaved by Meyer (or El Destructo, as he prefers to be called) and his charms, lovely women who are allowed to serve him until he becomes bored and moves on to his next trifle.

Recently, as we were being catered to by the latest Missy, a striking young Asian woman with blond hair, Meyer finally divulged to me the whole of his sick, insane, vengeful plan. The riches he has massed from the Basic Instructions Empire, the millions of dollars of wealth he has stock-piled from the generous rewards of drawing comic strips, has been focused into one awful enter-prise: the creation of what he calls a Great Cosmic Shoe, a piece of footwear of such enormous proportions that with one stomp it will wipe out the entire existence of his hometown. When I asked him what giant foot would wield this enormous shoe, he only became more enraged, and I felt it best to drop the whole matter.

It was no use trying to reason with him, spittle playing on his chin, his sweaty bald pate glowing in the fluorescent lighting of his basement. I knew he was serious and unwavering. This would be his Armageddon, a plan even more heinous than his attempt to defluoridate the water of Sunnyside and thus doom its inhabitants to a lifetime of poor oral hygiene.

Now, dear reader, the future is in your hands. Will you continue to purchase "Basic Instructions" merchandise and send a small American town to its assured doom, or will you cast away this in-strument of evil and move on to more wholesome pursuits?

Burn this book before it is too late for all of us.

In strength,

RS

PUBLISHER
MIKE RICHARDSON

EDITOR
TIM ERVIN

DESIGNER
KRYSTAL HENNES

ART DIRECTOR
LIA RIBACCHI

MADE WITH 90% RECYCLED ART
A Collection of Basic Instructions™ Volume 2 by Scott Meyer

Published by
Dark Horse Books
A division of Dark Horse Comics, Inc.
10956 SE Main Street
Milwaukie, OR 97222

First edition: June 2010
ISBN 978-1-59582-505-6

10 9 8 7 6 5 4 3 2 1
Printed by Midas Printing International, Ltd., Huizhou, China.